GREEK TRADITIONAL MUSIC FOR ACOUSTIC GUITAR

MB20780

BY DUSAN BORJANIC

GW00656025

BILL'S MUSIC SHELF

© 2010 BY MEL BAY PUBLICATIONS, INC., PACIFIC, MO 63069.
ALL RIGHTS RESERVED. INTERNATIONAL COPYRIGHT SECURED. B.M.I. MADE AND PRINTED IN U.S.A.
No part of this publication may be reproduced in whole or in part, or stored in a retrieval system, or transmitted in any form
or by any means, electronic, mechanical, photocopy, recording, or otherwise, without written permission of the publisher.

Visit us on the Web at www.melbay.com or www.billsmusicshelf.com

Table of Contents

Author's Comment

"Greek Traditional Music for Acoustic Guitar" is a selection of 18 popular traditional Greek songs and dances arranged for acoustic guitar. Working on the adaptation of these traditional songs, I tried to keep to the authentic melodies and rhythm structure. I even took one step further by creating harmony structure of vocal version but preserved original phrases and scale runs, I also tried to adapt folk guitar technique in my versions of these songs.

In addition to these traditional songs, there are seven original compositions in popular *Laiko* style (bouzuoki music) created in an aim to confirm the great guitar potential as string instrument.

These original compositions are dedicated to Mr. William A. Bay.. I would like to thank Mr. Bay for all his support and help in realizing this project of mine. It is due to Mr. Bay's efforts that this project has gone ahead. I appreciate all his support and help.

Dusan

Introduction

Greece and Greeks

As one of the Mediterranean countries, Greece is a country of strong national identity with a majority of Greeks practicing Orthodox religion, which they seen to preserve at no matter what cost. Having as its close neighbors, Turkey to the east, Macedonia to the north and Albania at the north-east end, Greek borderline is not free from pressures of territorial changes. On one side there is still a concern about a mighty Turkish army. On the other side exist real Albanian supporters for greater Albania and Macedonian separatists all wishing to see some parts of Greece as their own rightly enlarged territory.

These days, Greek communities can be found all over the world and with the migrating process starting in the 20th century, Greeks have managed to make their homes as far as Australia and America, either for economic or political reasons.

Greek Music

Thanks to the geographical location of the country, Greek music is quite a fusion between East and West. Already in old traditional songs maintained in Eastern flavored minor scales, one can hear both Turkish and Iranian influence as well as religious chants dating back to the times of Byzantium. This is also evident in *Rebetica*, a kind of blues-sounding music very popular in 20 and 30. But it becomes mush more problematic when trying to discuss the origin of Greek instruments or religion! Although it is known that similar traditional instruments were at the time to be found throughout the entire Islamic world, no musicologist can say today for certain whether Arabs, Byzantines or Persians had first constructed them. There is not even any definite answer to the question how they spread. Also the fact of Greece being in close proximity to Italians, Albanians and some of the Slavic countries resulted in vast and extremely varied both local and national traditions, cherished today in music and dance. Again, owing to the geography of Greece one can distinguish two main groups when describing its music. These are mainland and music of the isles.

Mainland Music

The fact of Greece being part of the Ottoman Empire from the 14th century until its declaration of independence four hundred years late meant that folk music, which always kept history alive, was associated in the first place with fighting for independence. The instrumentation of these songs consisted often of clarinet *(klarino*, which reached the country in 1830s) and one more instrument which could be guitar, lauto, lautochitara or violin. From time to time lap drum or tambourines were added to emphasize the rhythm. This could be either in style of *Kalamatiano* or *Syrto*.

Kalamatiano

With the very name originating from the southern Peloponnesus' town called *Kalamata*, this dance can be vary often seen and heard during main festivities; traditional weddings, baptisms as well as popular village fiestas. Similarly to some other country dances it is danced in an open circle chain, but with time signature 7/8 (3+2+2/slow quick-quick). Throughout the years *Kalamatiano* became a national dance.

Tsamico (Roumeli)

Quite unusually, the roots of the name *Tsamico* lead to the clothing used by Greek worriers (so called *Klepths*) fighting against Turko–Albanian forces in the mountains during long years of Turkish occupation. It was danced by a group of men leaping high into the air to show off their bravery, courage and value as excellent fighters. Maintained in 3/4 times signature, it was danced originally by men only.

Syrto

The oldest of all Greek dances, *Syrto* uses the same dance steps as *Kalamatiano*, although has a different time signature 2/4. To quote Greek themselves when dancing *Syrto* one experiences not only the simple enjoyment of following the steps and the music, but also a rare sense of human continuity. It has been now more than 2000 years since Greeks indulged in cultivating it.

Maciej Raginia
London, 26th January
2006

Symbol and Technique Explanation

Arrows

a) $\uparrow$ = downstroke   b) $\downarrow$ = upstroke
(i)   *(i)*

c) $\downarrow$ $\uparrow$ = down and upstroke arpeggio
     (p)   *(a)*

d) = down/up arpeggio
(p) (i) (m) (a)

Rasgueado

a) = triplet rasgueado
     (p) (m) (p)

b) = 4 beats rasgueado
     (e) (a) (m) (i)

c)  = continue rasgueado

(e   a   m   i   e   a   m   i   e   a   m   i   e   a   m   i)

Percussion

a) $\times$ = tap (on to sondboard)   b) Ⓢ = slap (on to soundboard)

Strings

        E   B   G   D   A   E

Frets

   I   II   III   IV   V   VI   VII   VIII   IX   X.........etc.

Right hand fingers

        (p)   =   thumb

        (i)   =   index

        (m)   =   middle

        (a)   =   ring

        (e)   =   little

Left hand fingers

        1   =   index

        2   =   middle

        3   =   ring

        4   =   little

Left hand fingers

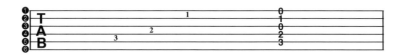

Instructions on Music and Technique

Notation and Tablature

The music is written in standard notation and tablature.

Six horizontal lines of the tablature represent six strings of the guitar.

The number on the tablature lines refer to positions on the fingerboard where tones are to be produced.

O = open string (a tone produced without pressure of the left hand finger)

Fingering

Left hand fingers:

1 = index finger

2 = middle finger

3 = ring finger

4 = little finger

Right hand fingers:

(p) = thumb

(i) = index finger

(m) = middle finger

(a) = ring finger

(e) = little finger

Explanation of Symbols

The symbols used in this book constitute standard symbols which appear throughout different methods for guitar referring to varied musical styles.

Graphic Explanation

Arrows:

= down stroke (from bass to treble strings)

= up stroke (from treble to bass strings)

= down stroke arpeggio (from bass to treble)

= up stroke arpeggio (from treble to bass)

Percussion:

$\times$ = tap onto the soundboard with the right hand ring finger

O = slap onto the soundboard with the pad of the right hand finger

Application of Technique

Example No. 1 ("Diamond Ring")
Page no. 4
Bars no. 50 and 51
Suggested right hand fingering
For playing rasgeado

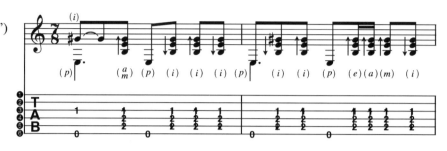

Bar no. 165
Suggested right hand fingering
For playing melody notes

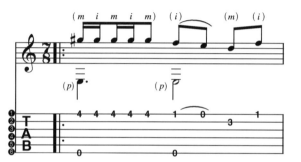

Example no. 2 ("O Ilios")
Bars no. 2 and 3
Characteristic rhythm pattern
for Tsamiko dance.
Suggested right hand
rasgeado formula

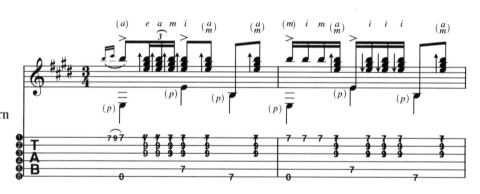

Example no. 3 ("Mori Kakia Gitonisa")

Bar no. 1 (Percussion)
Tap onto single bass string
Than onto melodic strings
Tap with outside part of the thumb near the bridge

Bar no. 4
Tap onto soundboard with the top of the right hand ring *(a)*

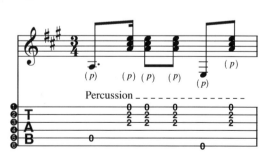

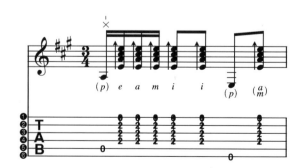

10

Example no. 4 ("Dio Mavra Matia Aapo")

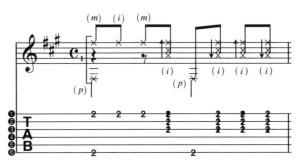

Page no. 1
Bar no. 1 (percussion-pizzicato)
Symbol ($\times$) on the notes system indicate that are played dumped strings. Touch the string with left finger over the fret where note has to be played.

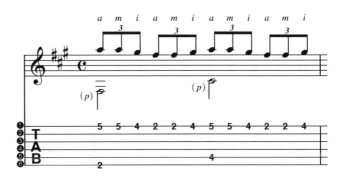

Bar no. 5
Characteristic pattern for playing melody lines in East European folk music. Suggested right hand formula is ($a\ m$ I)

Example no. 5 ("O diosmos ke o vasilicos")

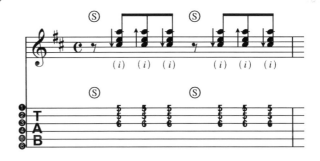

Page no. 11
Bar no. 103 (percussion)
Slap onto soundboard with the pad of right hand fingers.

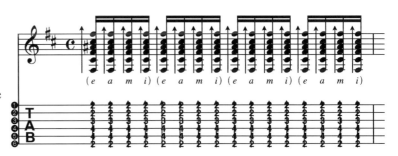

(continue rasgeado)
Four downstroke rasgeado played with the following fingers ($e\ a\ m\ i...$)

11

O Ilios
(Tsamico)

Arranged by Dusan Borjanic

Traditional
(Greece)

13

14

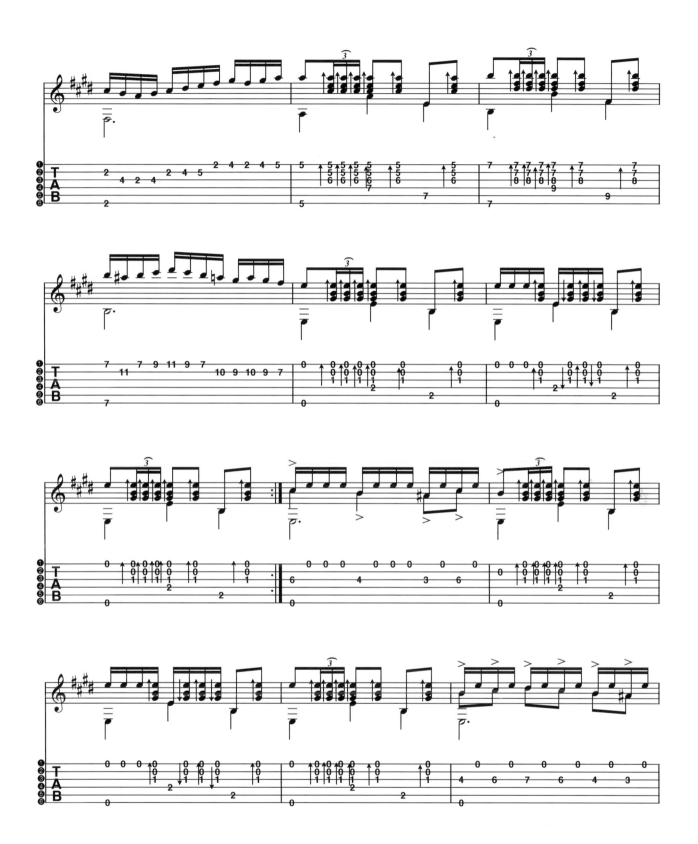

15

Mori Kakia Gitonisa

(Tsamico)

Arranged by Dusan Borjanic

Traditional
(Greece)

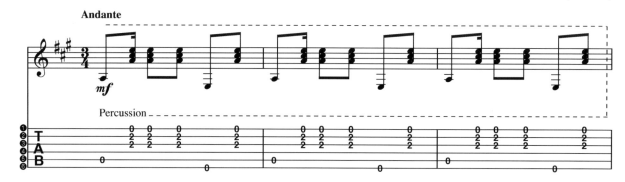

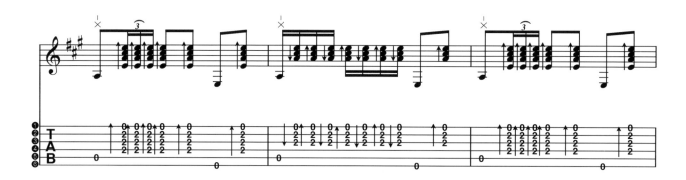

21

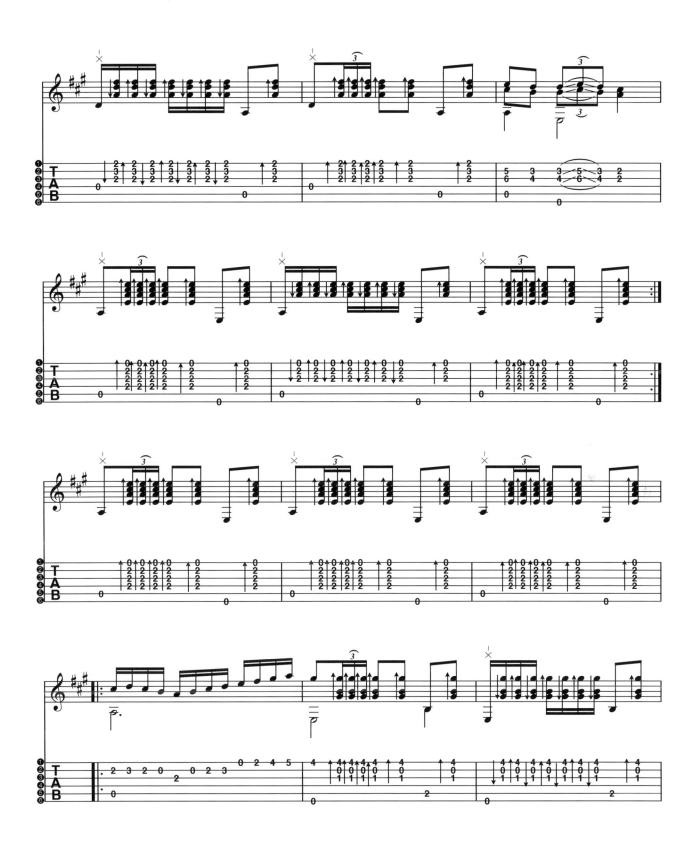

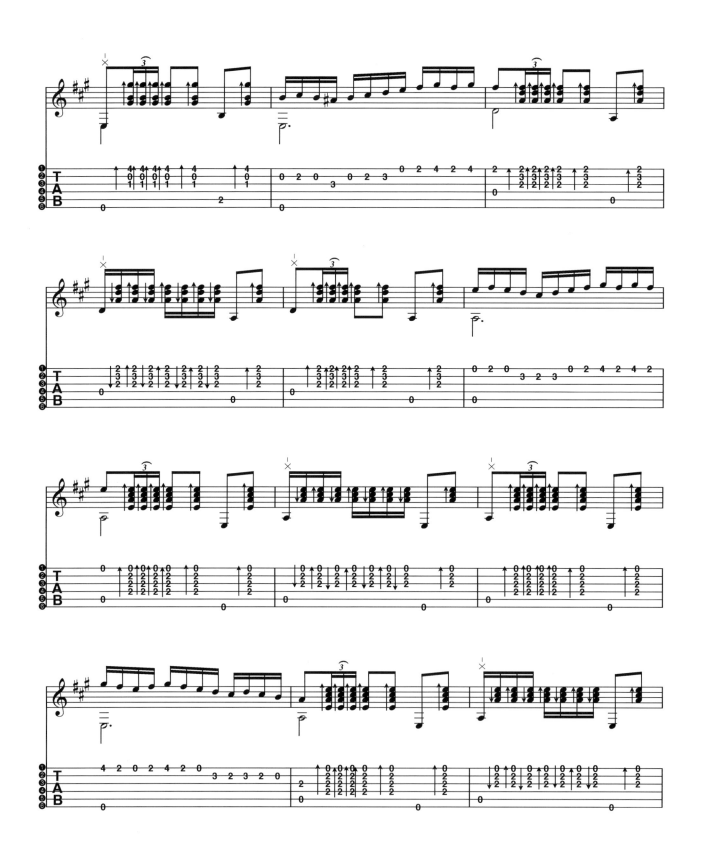

24

26

Diamandi Dahtilidi

(Kalamatiano)

Arranged by Dusan Borjanic

33

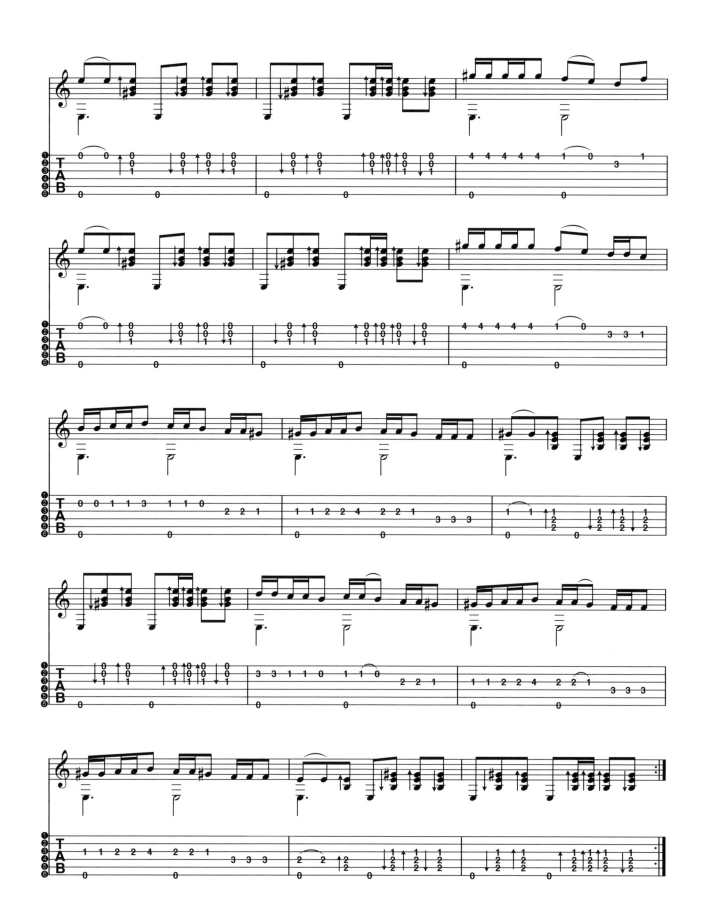

Ston Adi Ta Katevo

(Kalamatiano)

Arranged by Dusan Borjanic

**Traditional
(Greece)**

45

47

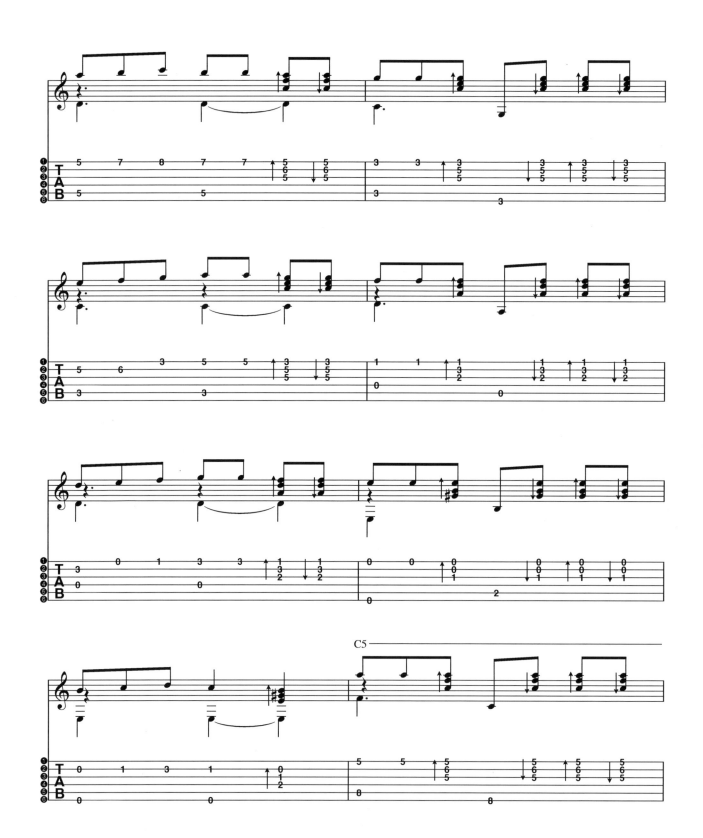

50

a) Diamando Pios Se Filise
b) Beno Mes T Abeli

(Kalamatiano)

Arranged by Dusan Borjanic

Traditional (Greece)

Ti Na Se Kano Galani

(Kalamatiano)

Arranged by Dusan Borjanic

Traditional
(Greece)

57

60

Dio Mavra Matia Agapo

(Sirta)

Arranged by Dusan Borjanic

Traditional
(Greece)

O Diosmos Ke O Vasilikos

(Syrto)

Arranged by Dusan Borjanic

Traditional
(Greece)

poco a poco accel.

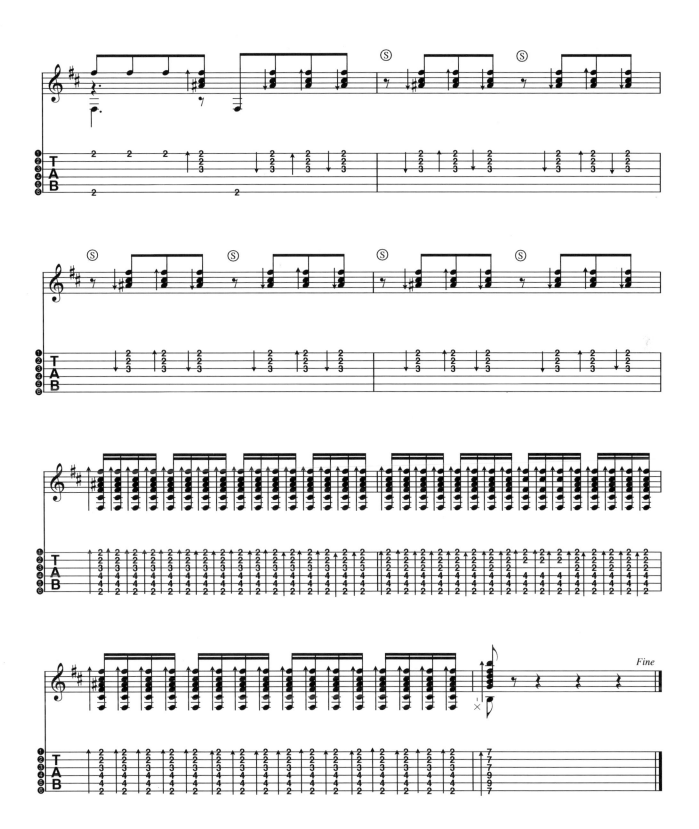

a) Orea Pou Ine I Nifi Mas
b) Simera Labi O Ouramos

Arranged by Dusan Borjanic

(Kalamatiano)

**Traditional
(Greece)**

90

Varante ta Clarina

(Kalamatiano)

Arranged by Dusan Borjanic

Traditional
(Greece)

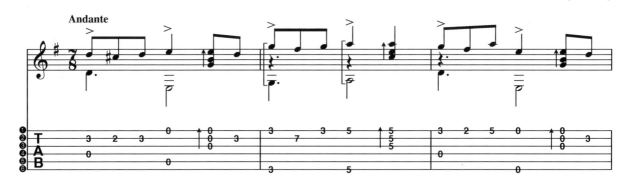

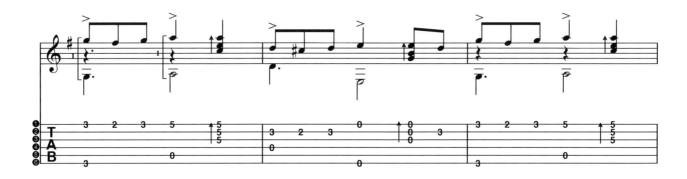

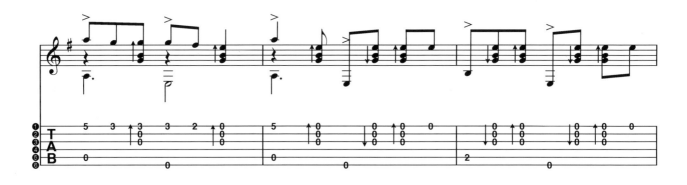

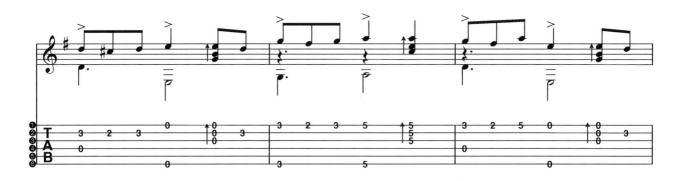

Simera Gamos Ginete

(Wedding Song)

Arranged by Dusan Borjanic

Traditional
(Greece)

Filim Kalos Orisate

(Kalamatiano)

Arranged by Dusan Borjanic

Traditional
(Greece)

Ise Agelos Oreos

(Kalamatiano)

Arranged by Dusan Borjanic

Traditional (Greece)

O Amarantos

(Tsamico)

Arranged by Dusan Borjanic

Traditional (Greece)

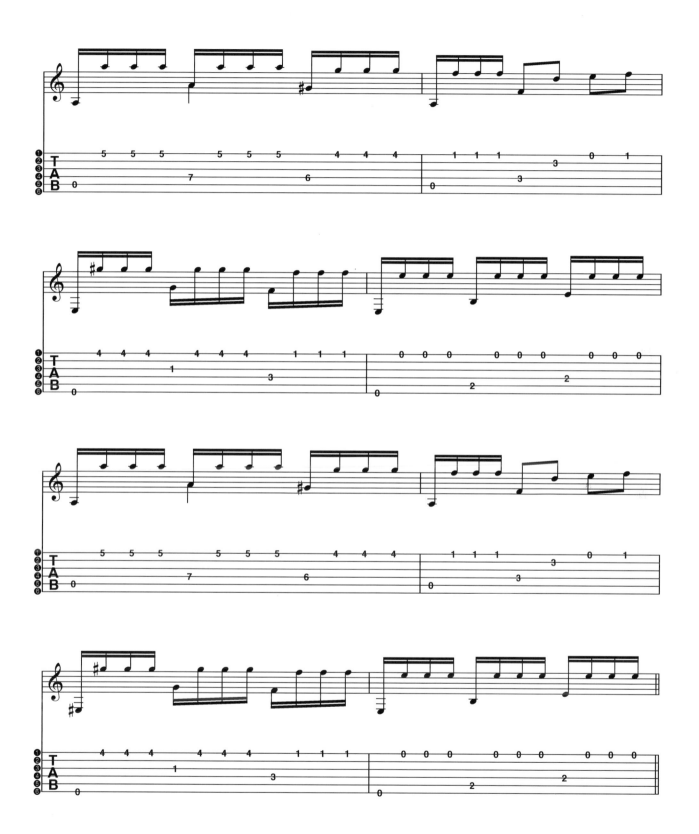

Me Gelasan Mia Haravgi

Arranged by Dusan Borjanic

Traditional
(Greece)

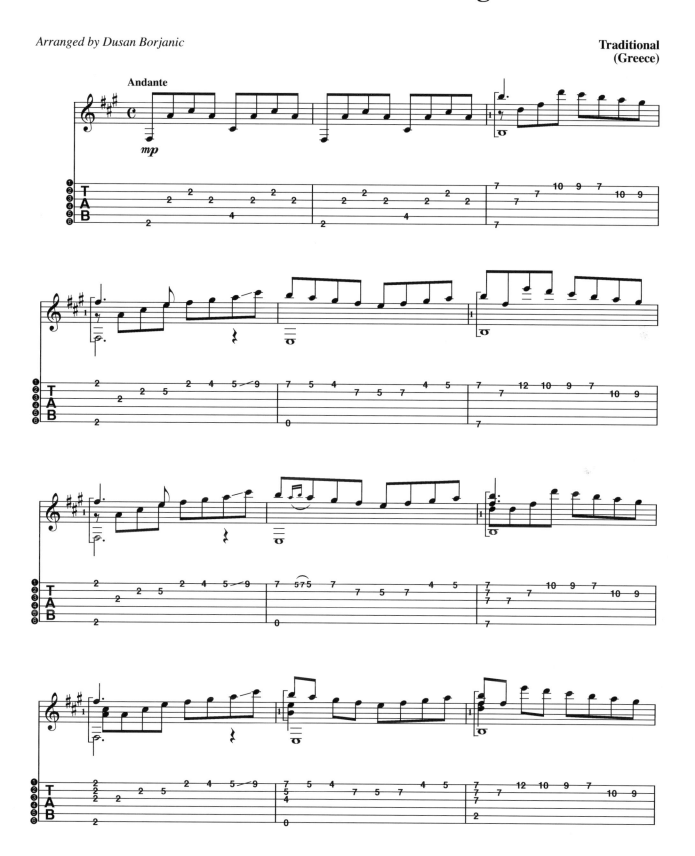

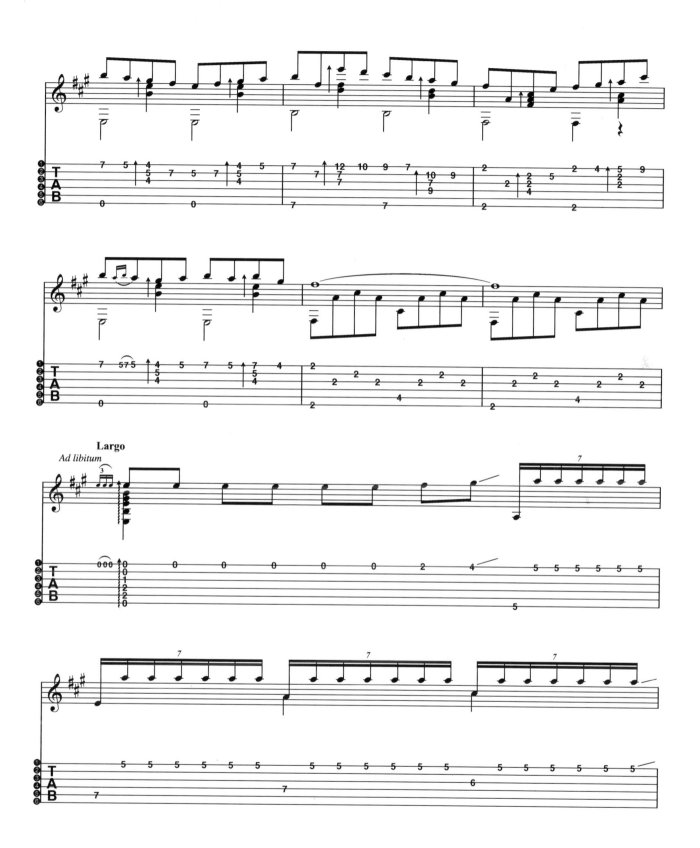

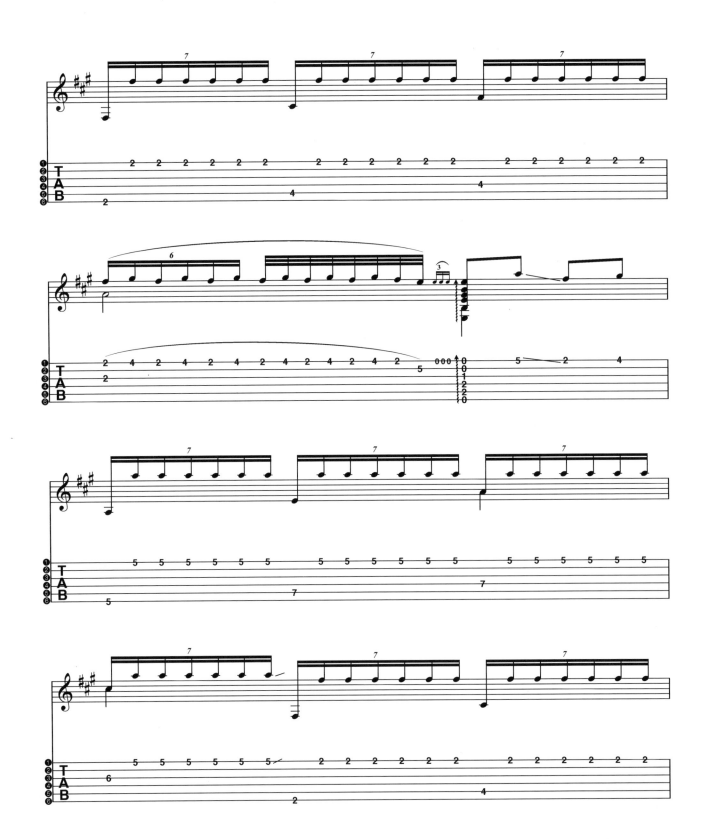

124

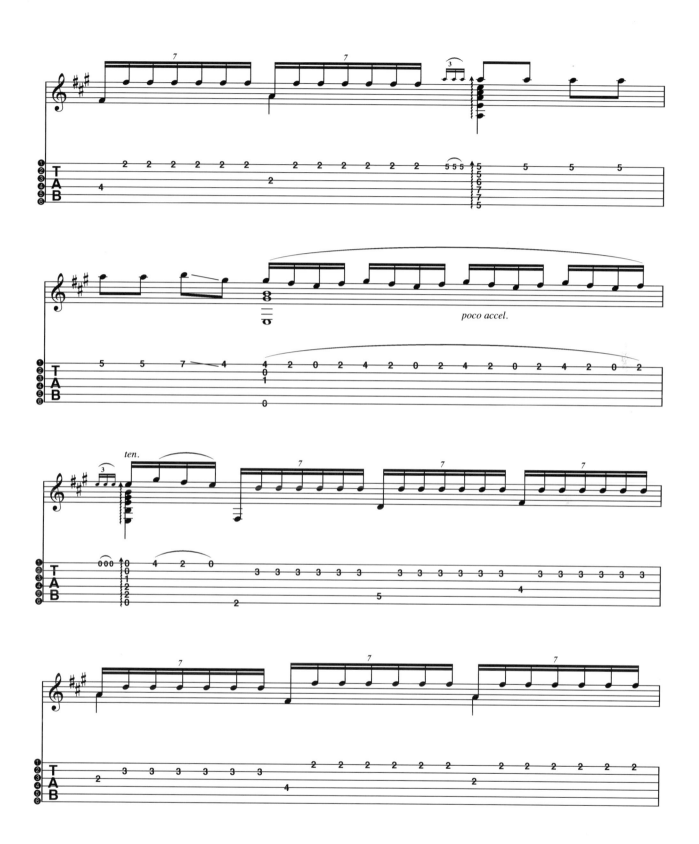

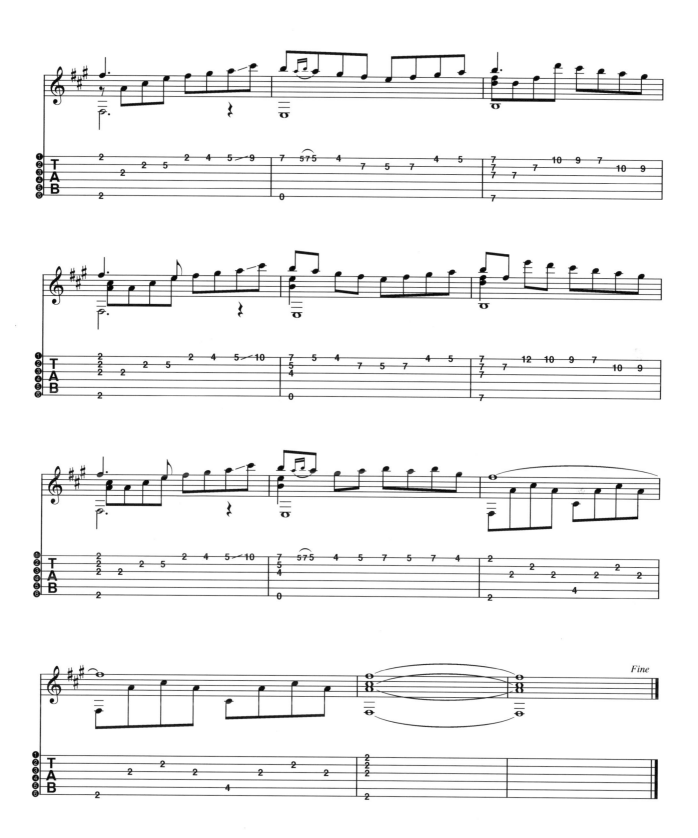

I Vlaha I Omorfi

Arranged by Dusan Borjanic

Traditional
(Greece)

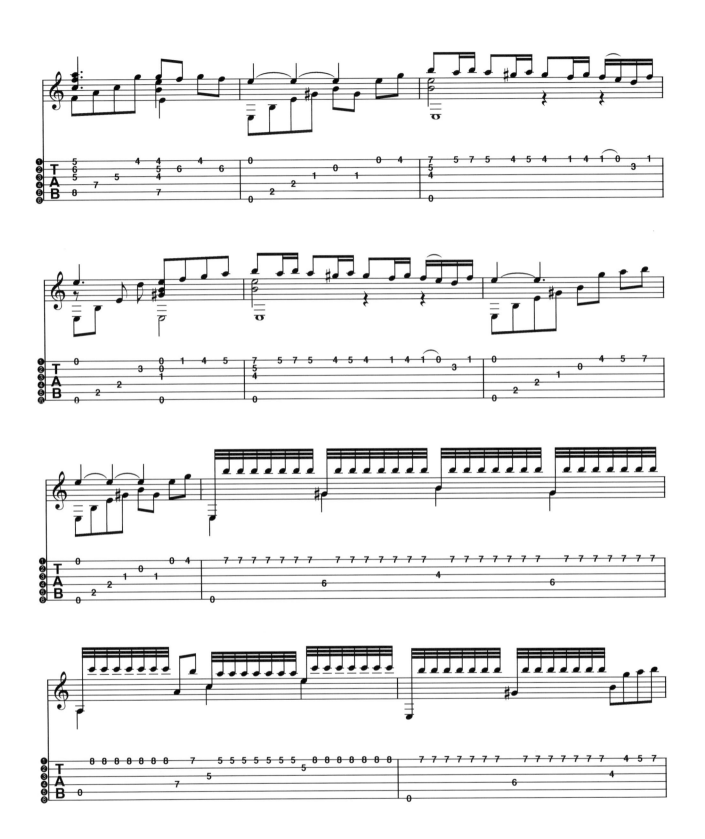

poco a poco rit.

pp

Fine

132

Giurgia

(Sirta)

Arranged by Dusan Borjanic

Traditional (Greece)

138

139

141

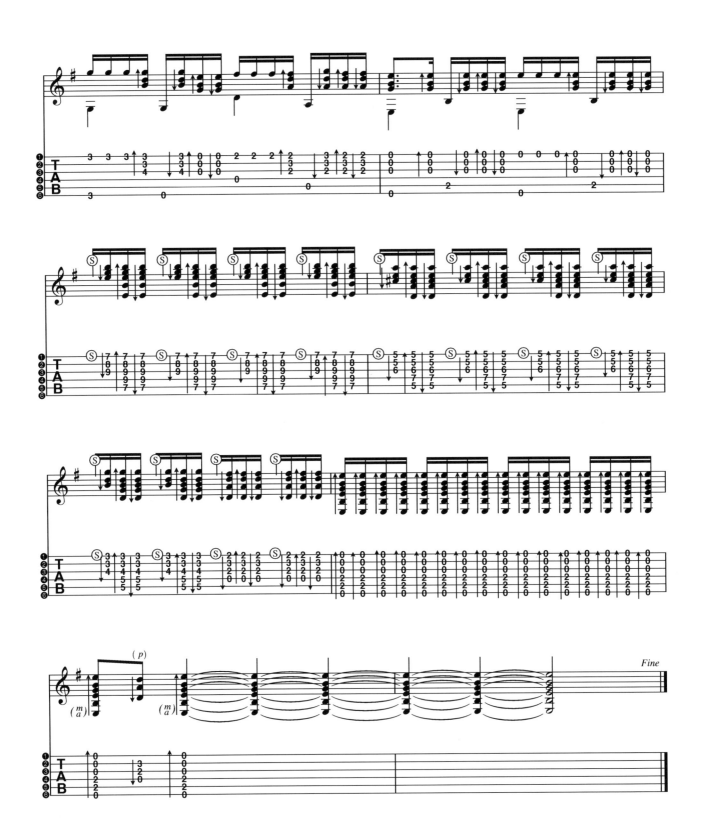

Egiotisa

(Kalamatiano)

Arranged by Dusan Borjanic

Traditional
(Greece)

143

144

145

149

To Mr. William A. Bay

No. 3 Athens Souvenirs

Music by Dusan Borjanic

150

151

To Miss Maria Kapotai

Maria

(Kalamatiano)

Music by Dusan Borjanic

155

To Mr. William A. Bay

No. 4 Mediteranean Dance

Music by Dusan Borjanic

160

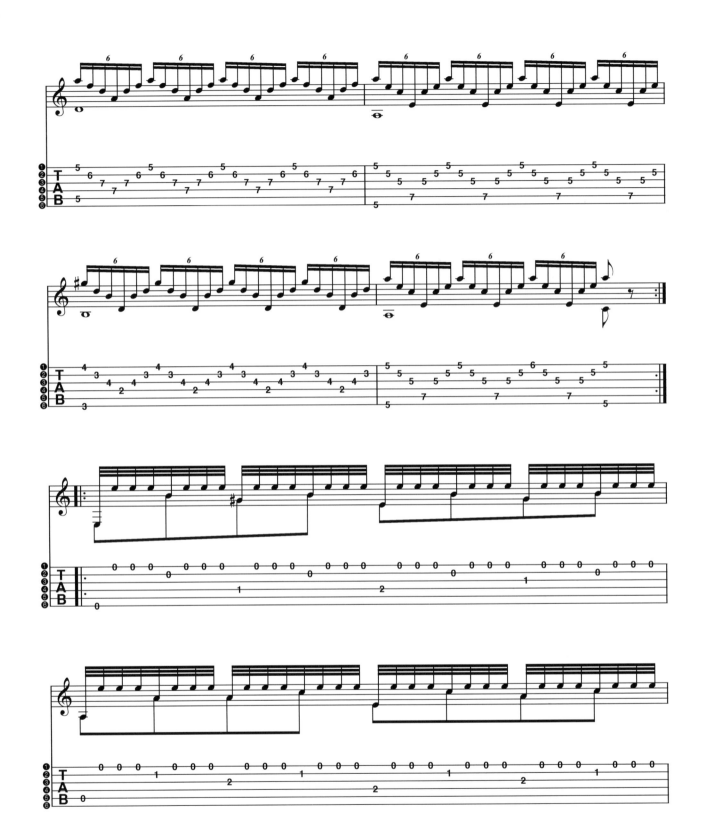

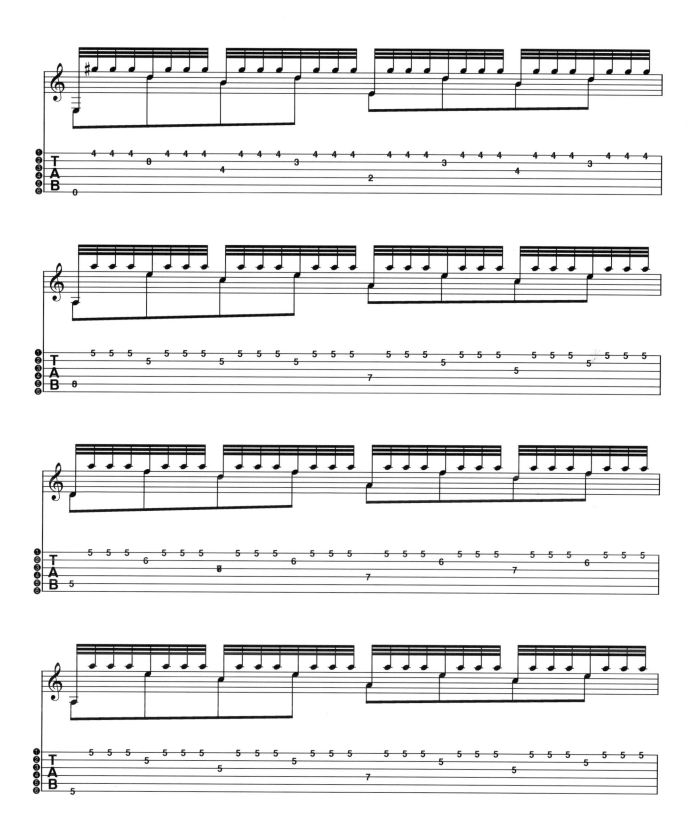

163

To Mr. William A. Bay

No. 2 Nostalgia

Music by Dusan Borjanic

166

170

To Mr. William A. Bay

No. 1 Oriental

Music by Dusan Borjanic

172

175

177

179

To Mr. William A. Bay

Greek Dance I

Music by Dusan Borjanic

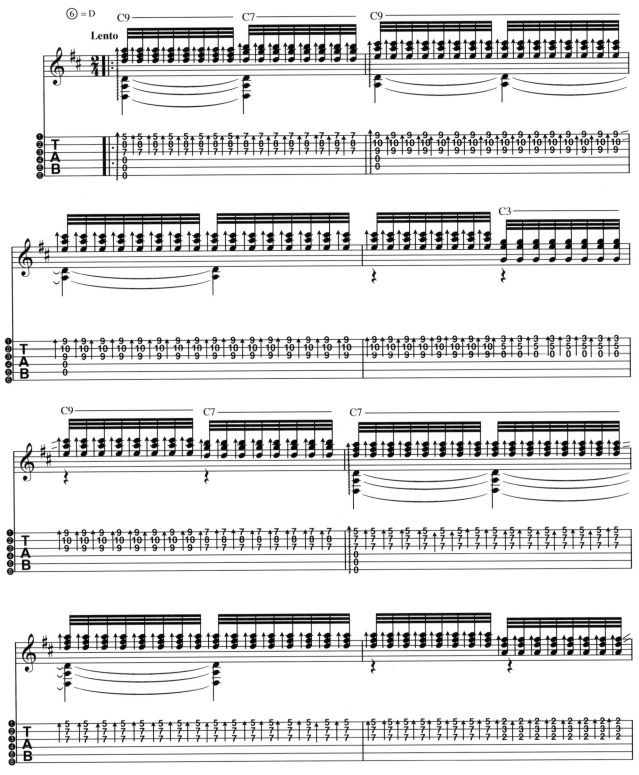

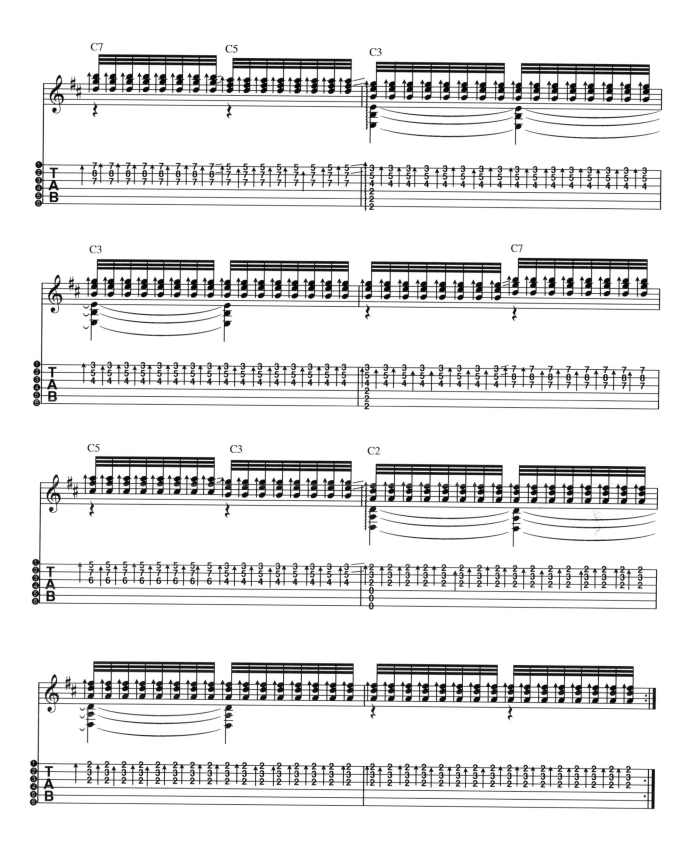

181

184

185

188

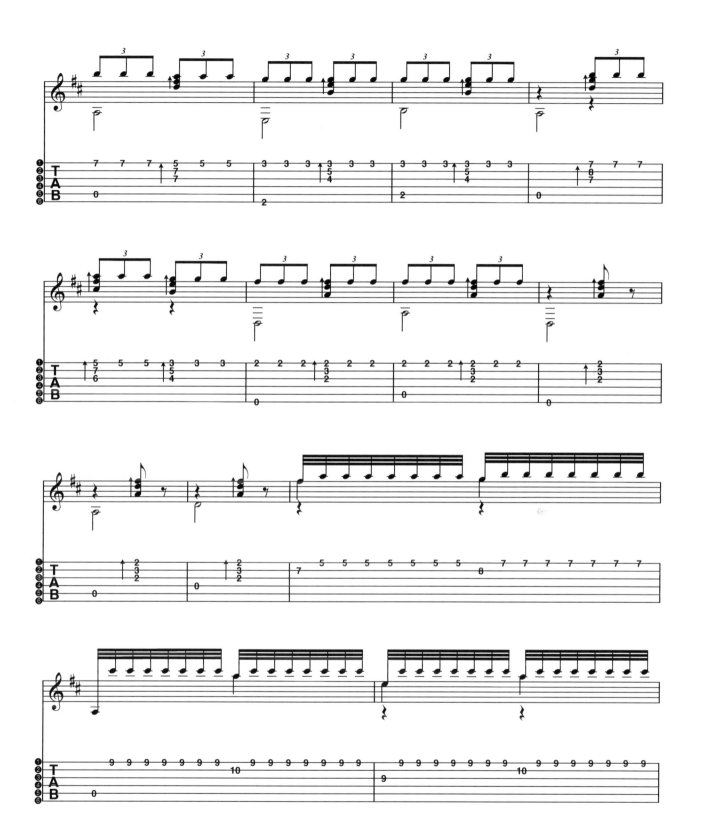

189

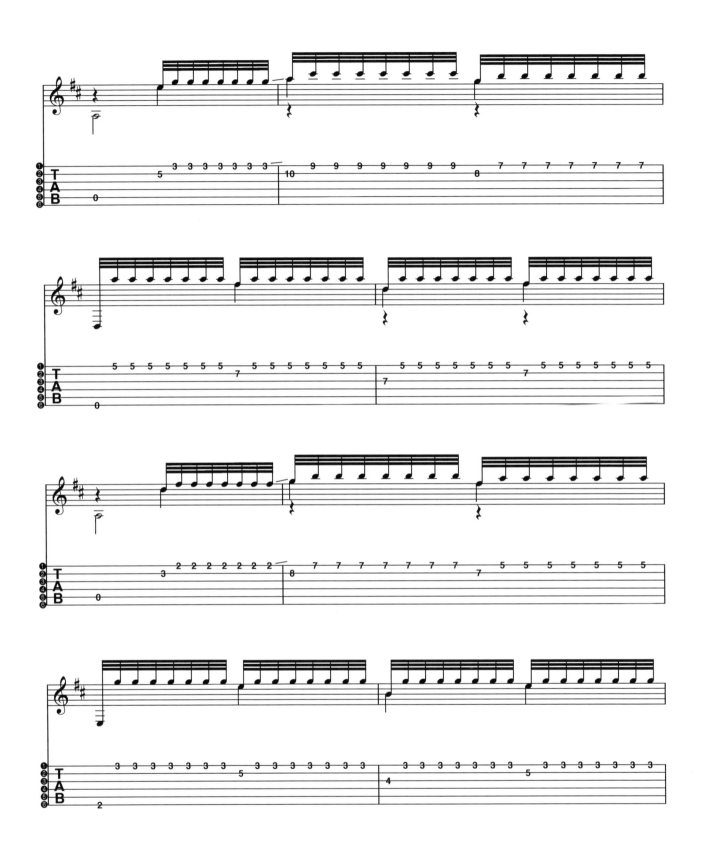

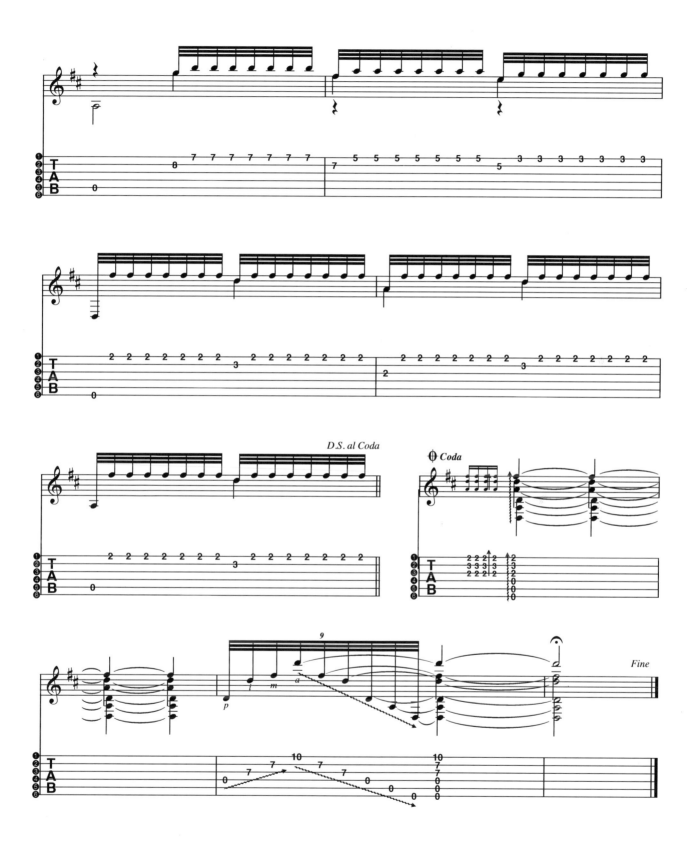

To Mr. William A. Bay

Greek Dance II

Music by Dusan Borjanic

193

194

195

197

Author's Biography

Dusan Borjanic-guitarist, teacher and composer- was born on October 20, 1947 in Zemun, a city in the former Yugoslavian Republic of Serbia. He started music education at an early age of 10, receiving lessons in accordion and music theory. In his teens he began the study of classic guitar. He studied with Professor Nada Kondic for many years and completed his formal education at the music school "Jovan Bandur" in Pancevo City near Belgrade. Also, Dusan worked as a private teacher in Belgrade for many years. He performed actively all along the Adriatic coast.

In 1992 Dusan came to England due to the civil war in Yugoslavia. While in London he studied flamenco guitar under Juan Martin. During his stay in London, Dusan broadened his musical interestests to include World and Folk music genres.

In 2009 Dusan completed full time course work and received a diploma in Music Technology and Theory from the Working Men's College in London.

UNIQUELY INTERESTING MUSIC!

Printed in Great Britain
by Amazon

35066370R00115